92   Knudson, R. Rozanne 1932-
DID   Babe Didrikson :
         athlete of the century

DATE DUE

DEC. 1 0 1995			
DEC 2 4 '95			

NEW 10-93

92   Knudson, R. Rozanne 1932-
DID   Babe Didrikson :
         athlete of the century

DEMCO

BABE DIDRIKSON

ATHLETE OF THE CENTURY

BY R. R. KNUDSON

Illustrated by Ted Lewin

PUFFIN BOOKS

PUFFIN BOOKS

A Division of Penguin Books USA Inc.
375 Hudson Street   New York, New York 10014

Viking Penguin Inc., 40 West 23rd Street, New York, New York 10010, U.S.A.
Penguin Books Ltd, Harmondsworth, Middlesex, England
Penguin Books Australia Ltd, Ringwood, Victoria, Australia
Penguin Books Canada Limited, 2801 John Street, Markham, Ontario, Canada L3R 1B4
Penguin Books (N.Z.) Ltd, 182–190 Wairau Road, Auckland 10, New Zealand

First published by Viking Penguin Inc. 1985
Published in Puffin Books 1986
5   7   9   10   8   6
Text copyright © R. R. Knudson, 1985
Illustrations copyright © Ted Lewin, 1985
All rights reserved

Printed in U.S.A.
Set in Garamond #3

"Women of Our Time" is a registered trademark of Viking Penguin Inc.

Library of Congress Cataloging in Publication Data
Knudson, R. Rozanne,   Babe Didrikson, athlete of the century.
Reprint. Originally published: New York: Viking Kestrel, 1985.
Summary: A biography, emphasizing the early years, of Babe Didrikson, who
broke records in golf, track and field, and other sports, at a time when there
were few opportunities for female athletes.
1. Zaharias, Babe Didrikson, 1911–1956—Juvenile literature.   2. Athletes—
United States—Biography—Juvenile literature.   [1. Zaharias, Babe Didrikson,
1911–1956.   2. Athletes]   I. Lewin, Ted, ill.   II. Title.
[GV697.Z24K68   1985]   796'.092'4 [B]   [92]   85-43390   ISBN 0-14-032095-4

CONTENTS

BABE DIDRIKSON
ATHLETE OF THE CENTURY

1

An Athlete Finds Her Name

One day early in this twentieth century, a young girl was training to be the greatest all-around athlete the world has ever known. Her name was Mildred Ella Didrikson, and she was scrubbing the porch floor.

She had tied the scrub brushes to her feet. On these "skates" she dashed around in soap suds, whistling and singing. When she finished the floor, she washed all the porch windows. Round and round her hands sped. She must hurry. There were dishes to wash or dry, taking turns with her three sisters. And clothes to help Momma wash on a scrubbing board, then rinse in a big tub. And her three brothers' shirts must be ironed with a heavy iron.

If Mildred ducked outside to the hammock to play her harmonica, her momma called her back, for now it was time to go for the family groceries. Mildred ran to the store at top speed. She hurdled high over seven hedges in the neighbors' backyards. Quickly she gathered the food her momma had asked her to bring home. Holding the bag tightly she raced to a streetcar, trying to beat it from stop to stop along the street.

Children in that neighborhood of Beaumont, Texas, watched Mildred race. Some of them thumbed their noses and called her a "tomboy."

"Sissies," Babe hollered to them. Other children

rooted for Babe to beat the streetcar, to get home as fast as she could to play circus with them. Their circus was a trapeze hanging from a tree in the Didriksons' backyard. Mildred, her younger brother Arthur, her older sister Lillie, and their friends took turns swinging on it. In the backyard they also lifted weights—a barbell made from an old broomstick with flatirons at each end. They played marbles. They jumped all over a jungle gym built by Mildred's poppa.

Later these children ran off together to find sidewalks for roller skating and vacant lots for football games. When they ended their day with a swim in the Neches River, Mildred turned swimming into a race. She beat Arthur, Lillie, and their friends. She hated to lose.

In the evening, after Mildred had washed or dried the dishes, her poppa read sports news from his paper. He talked to his seven children about athletes of the times: Babe Ruth, Red Grange, Jack Dempsey. He explained about the World Series, about golf tournaments, and about the Olympic games. Mildred listened with all her might because she wanted to be a famous athlete herself. Each night before she went upstairs to bed, Mildred bragged that she would someday be just like the champions in her poppa's newspaper, wait and see.

Of course Mildred didn't understand that her housework and her childhood contests were shaping her into a champion. She was simply having fun, not training madly for the sports career that in fact was almost always beyond the reach of any girl in those days, especially a girl from a big family without money.

Money bought sports equipment. It paid for memberships in private country clubs, where coaches taught swimming "strokes," diving, golf, and tennis to rich girls. These were the acceptable competitive sports for young ladies, not the rowdy games Mildred played with such passion around her poor neighborhood in south Beaumont.

But Mildred wasn't going to need wealthy parents in order to excel in athletics. Her child's body was responding to the daily exercise of scrubbing, lifting, bending, carrying—movements that made her flexible and strong. Her constant motion built her stamina. Her natural speed increased from entering hundreds of races. The skating she did, the hurdling, the swinging, and the swimming developed her natural agility and coordination, as well as her sense of rhythm and balance. Mildred Didrikson was becoming a winner by leaps and bounds.

Her brain kept pace with her body. She grew up with a winner's mentality, which means she made winning the main goal in her childhood games, a goal to work hard for, to fight for if necessary. She was quick to use her fists if another player hit her first or insulted her when tempers flared in competition. The bruises she got in return were forgotten when games began again.

Mildred soon won all the marbles in her neighborhood. To do that, she had to beat boys. She beat them in other sports, too. She dared any boy to kick a football farther than she could or throw a baseball harder. Boys chose her among the first for their baseball teams because she hit home runs. They decided to call her "Babe" for their home-run hero, Babe Ruth.

That nickname stuck to Babe all her life.

She had been born in 1911 in Port Arthur, Texas. Her mother Hannah and her father Ole were Norwegian. They had emigrated to Texas to find a good life and they succeeded by making their family the joyful center of their lives. Ole Didrikson, a skilled professional carpenter, built their first house in Port Arthur. When a hurricane flooded it in 1915 and almost washed it out to sea, he moved the family inland to Beaumont. There he eventually bought a house and added rooms with his own hands. Hannah Didrikson spent her days taking care of her children. In Norway she had ice-skated and skied for fun. In hot, flat east Texas her pleasures came from such household tasks as cooking for her active children.

The most important nourishment Babe's parents gave her was their love. Because they loved her they accepted her differences, her independent ways. What did it matter if their Babe hated to wear frilly dresses like other girls? Momma and Poppa allowed her to wear their sons' old clothes. And why should they be troubled if Babe chose the harmonica in those days when playing it was considered tomboyish? They welcomed Babe into the family "orchestra" of singing voices, drums, and a violin. Momma welcomed Babe home from endless ball games by serving hot suppers good enough for any training table. Poppa cooked hot oatmeal with butter for breakfast. These healthful meals kept Babe in shape for competition.

Babe's parents loved her despite her devilish spirit. When Babe sneaked away from housework, her momma might bring her indoors by the ear. "Don't let that dirt in the corner laugh at you. Get it out, *min babe*," Momma would urge. But then she'd laugh along with Babe. Babe's wide smile and innocent blue eyes were hard to resist.

Poppa didn't spank Babe when she put soap on the streetcar tracks to make the streetcar slide and slither. She fast-talked—sweet-talked—her way out of punishment.

"It wasn't my brother, it was me, Poppa," she confessed. Poppa allowed Babe to hide from him under the porch.

Babe returned her parents' love and kindness. She was an affectionate child in an affectionate family. She showed her strong feelings by earning money to contribute to her momma's grocery fund, as did the other children. Babe and her brothers mowed lawns. Her sisters did baby-sitting for neighbors.

"I wanted to do things for Momma and Poppa," said Babe many years later. "They'd done so much for us."

During Babe's junior high school years, she worked part time in a fruit-packing plant and in a potato-sack factory. She sewed sacks for a penny apiece. She kept a few nickels of her money for movies and goodies. Naturally Babe sewed faster than others in the factory, sixty-eight sacks an hour. Her finger were strong and agile. Her vision was keen. Her eye–hand coordination had always been excellent. For those reasons alone Babe would have swiftly stitched up potato sacks.

Combine Babe's physical strengths with her winner's mentality, add the attraction of making money for her family as well as for herself—and Babe Didrikson could not fail in future competition.

2

The Most Valuable Player

Babe Didrikson learned to play basketball in Beaumont's Magnolia School. This elementary school had four outdoor courts and a gym inside, plenty of space for children to learn the basics of basketball. Babe worked on her shots at recess. She would also creep out of class when her teacher wasn't watching to shoot just one more basket, one more, and another. After school she had the chance to learn from older girls because both the junior high and high school girls' basketball teams came to Magnolia for practice. Babe stood on the sidelines, alert for ways to improve her own game. She chased down balls and zinged them back. She heckled the older girls to let her practice with their teams.

Not then, not ever, did Babe whine or beg to play. Instead she met her doubters head-on with her skill.

She challenged them to sink more foul shots in a row than she could. She teased them to sink two-handed baskets that she could put away with one hand. Babe usually made her shots, thus showing up anyone who dared to keep her from playing with them.

At South End Junior High, Babe made the girls' basketball team. She made it again in Beaumont High School. In fact she played on every girls' team in high school: volleyball, basketball, baseball, tennis, swimming, and golf. From now on Babe's whole school life would be sports.

She did only enough schoolwork to stay on the teams. Teammates were her only friends. Other girls—the popular crowd, the studious crowd—ignored Babe except when she was starring in sports for Beaumont High. In between games they called Babe a "freak." Babe still wore old, boyish clothes. Most high school girls wore girdles and stockings and high heels and lipstick. Babe wore her short brown hair straight with her bangs squared off severely. Most girls curled their hair in the fashion of those days. They lived for good grades and for dates with boys. High school boys never took Babe out on dates. When they talked to her at all, it was about sports. They thought Babe was a "toughie."

Any young girl would have suffered from being ignored or called names by popular students. Surely Babe suffered, although she never let on in the usual ways. She didn't fight back with her fists as she had as a child. She didn't change her style of dress in order to fit safely into the crowd. She didn't ask for pity. Far from it! She scorned the "sissygirls" as well as the boys who couldn't match her sports skills. Babe would rather be the best athlete in Texas and after that the best in the world than be an invisible student at Beaumont High. She fought back at others by bragging about herself.

"I can beat Raymond all to little bits and pieces at kicking," Babe told the boy's football coach about a player who kicked extra points. The boys' coach let Babe try—and she kicked farther and straighter than Raymond.

Babe fought back also by working hard on her skills. Her own coach called Babe the finest natural athlete she had ever worked with in high school, and the most coachable. Babe caught on immediately when an athletic move was explained to her. She asked endless questions to improve her moves, even seeking help from the boys' basketball coach. He sat Babe down to watch his team practice. She had talked her way out of study hall to get this extra coaching on her pivoting and passing. It paid off handsomely. With Babe in the lineup, *her high school basketball team never lost a game.*

In Texas in the 1920s, large crowds went to high school ball games. Babe made fans of people who recognized how skillfully she played her position. To them Babe was an aggressive scrambler on court, not a freak or toughie. She was the game-winning forward. That's what counted. Newspaper reporters sat up and took notice of their hometown girl. They wrote:

BEAUMONT GIRL STARS IN BASKETBALL GAME

Babe saved these newspaper headlines and the articles about herself. Her scrapbook and audience grew.

BEAUMONT GIRL STARS AGAIN

She was voted to be on the all-city and all-state teams.

Watching Babe from the crowd one night in February 1930 was a scout searching for outstanding players— Colonel Melvin J. McCombs. He had been in the U.S. Army but now worked for Employers Casualty, an insurance company in Dallas, Texas. This company sponsored a women's basketball team called the Golden

Cyclones, and Colonel McCombs had hopes of improving his team. The more often his players won, the more they would get their photos into Texas newspapers. The Golden Cyclones wore hot-orange uniforms with the company's name stitched in large letters across their shirts. Every time they played before a crowd, they helped sell insurance.

Down below him on the court that night Colonel McCombs saw a one-woman cyclone! There Babe was, only five feet seven inches tall, and scoring, scoring, scoring against a team of taller, bigger girls. She ran around them. She ran past them and through them, almost at will. Her ball control electrified Colonel McCombs, who rushed to recruit her when the game ended. He urged Babe to come to Dallas and play for his team—immediately.

Now here was Babe's big chance to continue her rise to fame as a basketball star in a time of very few chances for women players beyond high school. There were no basketball scholarships to colleges, no basketball competition at the Olympics, no professional basketball leagues for women. Babe knew that.

She wanted to grab Colonel McComb's offer. If only she could talk her parents into letting her drop out of school and move to Dallas.

Hannah and Ole Didrikson hated to let Babe leave home. She was their youngest daughter, still their baby even in high school. They'd miss Babe's lively, devilish ways. Their happy home would miss the constant tunes from Babe's harmonica, which, after years of practice, she played as skillfully as she played basketball. Hannah Didrikson wept when she thought of Babe's leaving. She needed Babe for company and for help with the heavy housework. Dallas seemed so far away. The Didriksons did not own a car to drive the 250 miles for visits.

On the other hand, Babe would be making a steady salary as a secretary at the insurance company. Some of her money she would send home. Her parents seemed never to have enough because Ole Didrikson was unwilling sometimes and unable other times to find work. Also Babe would use some of her salary for trips back to Beaumont.

Her parents let Babe go. Many years ago they had crossed the Atlantic Ocean to start fresh. Babe had to cross only a corner of Texas.

Right away in Dallas, Babe earned success in nearly all she did. With her fast hands and lots of practice she had won a high school typing contest, and here this skill came in handy. She typed letters in Colonel McComb's department. He found Babe a room in a boarding house and drove her to the office each day to save her carfare from her salary of $75 a month (excellent for a beginner then).

The Employers Casualty Company paid Babe to be a secretary, but her real job was to play winning basketball for the Golden Cyclones. The company could not pay Babe directly for being on the team because if she took money for being an athlete she automatically became a professional. That would have meant she couldn't play with or against amateurs (who took no money). And since there were next to no professional teams for women *in any sport,* Babe had to remain an amateur in order to compete. The Amateur Athletic Union (AAU), which controlled many sports, had made this rule and acted as a watchdog to see that no one broke it.

Most of the Golden Cyclones worked in Colonel McComb's office. Just before her first game with them, Babe announced she planned to play the position of forward on their team. Not just any forward, either.

"Star forward," she let the Cyclones know in her outspoken way.

They already had a star center forward, but that night Babe took over the position and scored 14 points. She scored 16 points two nights later and 36 points in a game she played after only three weeks in Dallas. She also won a Dallas free-shooting tournament by making 57 out of 65 shots.

BABE DIDRIKSON SCORES 210 POINTS IN 5 GAMES

This was the headline after Babe led her team to second place at the National AAU women's basketball tournament. Newspapers and coaches voted her an All-American player. Scouts came to see her with invitations to work for other companies next year during basketball season. They said they would give her a cash bonus and increase her salary. Babe was tempted. Her family always needed money.

Colonel McCombs would not let another company steal Babe Didrikson. He recognized her as an athletic genius, even though her me-first demands were beginning to cause trouble on his team. Other players resented Babe's special treatment: her extra time off, her extra coaching, and her raise in salary. She had become the company's pet project, and her teammates were jealous. Babe was a young woman in need of fatherly coaching, thought Colonel McCombs. He wanted to guide her sports career for her own sake as well as for Employers Casualty. So he found the perfect way to keep Babe from quitting his company and joining another.

On a spring day in 1930 he took Babe to a track meet. He felt she might be impressed by the medals given to winners for their *individual* efforts. He hoped she might respond to the challenges of the many different events by wanting to try some of them herself.

Babe had never been to a track meet before. She knew next to nothing about the events Colonel McCombs pointed to as they walked around the Southern Methodist University track watching male students compete. Babe even had to ask "What's this?" about a javelin lying on the ground. Colonel McCombs showed her how to toss it like a spear. Babe tried to toss it, but the heavy javelin slipped from her hand, raising a sore spot on her back. Nonetheless Babe kept trying. She was used to ignoring the pain that often went along with athletics.

The other events also interested Babe. She watched

a student sprinting down a runway to launch himself
into the long-jump pit of sand. That looked like fun.
She watched a student on the track who was sprinting,
then going over a hurdle, then sprinting again, hurdling again. Babe believed she could do that. Hadn't
she practiced on hedges at home in Beaumont? And
those men in the track infield heaving a ball of iron
(shot put) and throwing a flattened ball of iron (dis-
cus). Babe had been throwing balls all her life. How
much harder could it be to throw these metal things?

Back at the office the other Golden Cyclones showed
their interest in becoming a track team by volunteer-
ing for one event each.

"How many events are there in this track and field?"
Babe asked Colonel McCombs.

"Nine or ten."

"Well, I'm going to do them all," said Babe with her usual self-confidence.

The team began training at the university track after work. Babe had to learn new techniques of movement. From Colonel McCombs she learned to count and to time her steps approaching the long jump, the high jump, and the eight hurdles in her 80-meter hurdle event. Hitting the take-off point on the right foot caused a smooth jump. Colonel McCombs taught her the old scissors-style high jump, and when she had jumped as high as she could using that style, he taught her the newer western roll. He urged her higher and higher by promising chocolate sodas each time the crossbar stayed on its two supports after her jump. He knew how much Babe loved sweets.

"Practice makes perfect," Babe wrote in a letter back to Beaumont. She often continued to train after dinner. Alone she would run around her neighborhood in Dallas, lifting her knees, swinging her arms, just as she would in a sprint event. On moonlit nights she stayed out even longer.

Four gold medals were Babe's at the end of her very first track meet, and her winning points added up to help the Golden Cyclones take a team trophy. They elected Babe captain. They began traveling to AAU track meets around the South. At every one of these in the spring and summer of 1930, Babe took gold medals. She set Texas records, all-South records, and American records. If the baseball throw had been an international event, she would almost certainly have held the world record that summer with her throw of 268 feet at the national AAU track meet.

"I made me a bracelet out of the first ten gold medals that I got," Babe wrote to a newspaper reporter back in Beaumont. "Fix me up a good write up . . . a big headline," she suggested.

To top off her first track season, AAU officials told Babe that she was so good she couldn't miss being sent to Los Angeles as a member of the 1932 United States Olympic track team.

3

Olympic Gold, Silver, and Confetti

The Tenth Olympiad. Two summers away, but Babe Didrikson now set her goal. She would win as many track and field events as she could enter in Los Angeles. Meanwhile, except for brief vacations home in Beaumont, she worked and played for Employers Casualty in Dallas.

Babe starred as a power hitter for the Golden Cyclones softball team. She competed in doubles tennis with a Cyclone teammate. She gave exhibitions of springboard and platform diving at a Dallas swimming pool. Employers Casualty sponsored golf lessons for

Babe at the Dallas Country Club. In winters she again played basketball, leading the Cyclones to the AAU championship in 1931 and to the runner-up position in the winter of 1932. Both years she repeated as a basketball All-American. In summer track and field, she won her usual string of medals.

What Babe did not win those years was friends. Truthfully, she had never excelled when it came to making friends among her teammates and opponents. They hated her bragging, which seemed as natural to her as her sports talent. Babe herself said she was only "popping off," but her teammates grew more and more tired of her pushiness to get herself into newspapers and her constant harmonica playing.

"I could have broken the world record just like taking candy from a baby," Babe was fond of boasting. "Plenty of other teams want me."

Perhaps Babe had developed her bragging ability as the next-to-youngest child trying to gain attention in a large family. Later she used bragging as a way of getting back at people who insulted her or who she thought might insult her. To the Golden Cyclones Babe seemed arrogant and childish. They tried to ignore her.

But she was not to be ignored that summer of 1932. Babe was twenty-one and soon to go into track and field record books.

A shrewd idea of her coach, Colonel McCombs, put her many steps closer to lasting fame. Alone in his office, studying track records of women from all over the United States, he began comparing Babe to these women. He noticed that Babe stood a chance of taking enough points to win the AAU team trophy single-handedly. Thus Colonel McCombs would need to send only one Golden Cyclone to Illinois for the AAU meet in July: Babe, his one-woman team.

The AAU Nationals would also serve as the Olympic trials. Women who placed first, second, or third in their events in Illinois would go directly to Los Angeles to compete there in those same events.

Babe's speed events began even before she arrived at the AAU starting lines: Because she had been up all night with a stomachache and had overslept the morning of the Nationals, she had to jump into a taxi and race to the stadium while throwing on her track suit in the back seat. She arrived just in time for the opening ceremonies.

Each team was introduced over a loudspeaker. Most of these teams had fifteen athletes or more, and soon there were two hundred women on the field. Babe stood alone. Her team's name brought a mighty cheer from the crowd. Babe waved to her audience.

Then this Cyclone spent the next three hours hustling from event to event. Officials held up starting lines to wait for her, and they gave her extra minutes to rest between events. Babe's special treatment from officials made other competitors fighting mad. Babe made them madder by going around the infield bragging.

"I'm going to win everything I enter," she hollered.

She almost did. Babe's afternoon in Illinois has been called "the most amazing series of performances ever accomplished by an individual, male or female, in track and field history." And today, more than fifty years later, her accomplishment still seems the most amazing in track and field history.

1st place	Long Jump	17 feet 6 inches
1st place	80-Meter Hurdles (She ran 11.9 in her first heat, a world record.)	12.1 seconds
1st place	Javelin (This throw beat her own world record.)	139 feet 3 inches
1st place	Baseball Throw (This throw beat her own U.S. record.)	272 feet 2 inches
1st place	Shot Put	39 feet 6 1/4 inches
1st place	High Jump (This was a tie with Jean Shiley. Both jumped this world-record height.)	5 feet 3 3/16 inches
4th place	Discus	

In the 100-yard dash Babe missed qualifying for the finals after advancing to a semifinal race.

SUPERGIRL, said sports pages across America the next day. Babe had scored 30 points to win the national championship for the Cyclones. The second-place team, with twenty-two members, scored only 22 points. Reporters covering the meet predicted "their" Babe would lead the U.S. track women to glory in the Los Angeles Olympics.

Fifteen women had gained places on the U.S. Olympic track team along with Babe. They were soon on their way from Illinois to California aboard a train together. They played cards, gossiped, read, and looked out the windows. Except energetic Babe. Even traveling across the country she continued her workouts. She exercised in the train's aisles. She stretched her legs on the tops of seats, preparing for hurdles. To keep her speed and stamina she ran the whole length of the train several times a day. Passengers became spectators, saying "Here she comes again" as Babe spurted by them.

"I'm the greatest. No one's better than me," Babe would shout.

Her teammates asked Babe to "take it easy" on the train. They asked her to stop showing off her AAU medals, stop putting ice down their backs, and, please, stop her pillow fights. Pillow feathers dusted their private train car from Babe's powerful blows. To prove to Babe what they really thought of her, the team elected another woman for their captain. They had decided that Babe was too "obnoxious" to be their leader.

Babe shrugged off her teammates' criticism. How could she reach her goals in Los Angeles if she let their words flatten her? Besides, as soon as the train pulled into the Los Angeles station Babe collided with a new audience, one that was eager to hear any zany thing she said.

An army of reporters flocked to Babe. They found her a fresh, open young woman who would answer their silliest questions. They encouraged her to rave on and on about every "great" thing she had done since she took her first baby step. She made their stories more interesting than their usual ones about modest athletes. Babe was "hot copy" all over the world.

"Yep, I'm going to win the high jump Sunday and set a world record. I don't know who my opponents are and, anyways, it wouldn't make any difference."

Reporters followed Babe back to her hotel. Two hundred women athletes from dozens of countries were also staying there but none of these got the attention Babe did. Reporters even asked about Babe's "beauty diet."

"I eat anything I want," she told them without a hint of modesty. Babe was proud of her lean, muscular body. She also told about her hurdling style. The Olympic coach wanted her to change it, but she wasn't going to, no, not her.

TEXAS TORNADO
TERRIFIC TOMBOY

Sports fans coast to coast fell in love with Babe. She had as much appeal as a movie star there in Los Angeles in the summer of 1932. In fact, movie stars wanted to meet Babe. She laughed at the jokes of Will Rogers and Clark Gable but they didn't laugh back at her claim that she had come to California to "beat everyone in sight." They believed Babe.

To beat everyone in sight! First of all, Babe Didrikson had to get through the opening Olympic cere-

monies in the Coliseum. Speeches and music and the Olympic oath seemed to take forever while 1,980 athletes roasted in the hot California sun. Babe couldn't have been more uncomfortable. Her U.S. uniform included itchy stockings, which she hated to wear, and shoes that pinched her feet. She ended up barefoot. She stood there wishing it were already time for her first event. She would rather be throwing her javelin.

The next day shadows had fallen at Los Angeles Coliseum by the time the javelin throwers were called to their infield places. Babe's main competition, the German women, began warming up by heaving their javs into the ground.

Babe usually tossed her javelin into the air in the very same motion she would use to make her three official attempts at distance. But today, far too many women crowded the javelin area to risk hitting any-one. So Babe competed without warming up her muscles. On her first attempt she felt the shoulder of her throwing arm pop. She knew she had injured it. The javelin flew 143 feet 4 inches, a new world record. Babe, however, was done for the day. If any other woman threw farther, Babe would not be able to out-distance her with the two throws she had left.

But no one beat Babe's first throw. She won a gold medal for the javelin and had a day off to rest before her next event, the 80-meter hurdles. There was not any possibility her shoulder would heal in one day—or even in one month. Babe would feel the soreness and stiffness for many months to come. But she competed in the hurdles anyway. She used both arms to power herself off the starting line. She swung them high for speed between hurdles. As she leaped the hurdles, she lifted her arms in rhythm with her legs.

In her first heat of the 80-meter hurdles, Babe set a world record of 11.8 seconds. (A heat is a trial race to decide which of the many runners will compete in the finals. Heats are run because there are only ten lanes on the track to decide a final winner.) In the finals Babe came from behind to snatch a gold medal at the finish line in 11.7 seconds, another world record.

Babe's two short steps to the top of the Olympic games winners' platform were becoming a habit. She planned to return once again after her final event, the high jump. To win she would have to outjump her American teammate, Jean Shiley, as well as outjump

a strong German contender. Would Babe be the first woman ever to go home with three Olympic gold medals in track and field?

Only Jean Shiley and Babe were left in the competition when the high-jump bar was raised to 5 feet 5 1/4 inches the next day. Babe sailed up and over, setting a new world record. Jean then cleared that height, equaling the record.

They were tied for first place. Judges had to raise the bar again to give each of them another chance to break their tie. At the height the judges chose—5 feet 6 1/2 inches—Jean took her turn and missed. Babe soared over the bar.

"I felt like a bird. Like looking down from the top of the Empire State Building," Babe said years later about this jump.

But as Babe landed in the high-jump pit, her foot kicked a sidepost that held the crossbar, causing the bar to fall. Judges decided she had missed her attempt. They lowered the bar and asked each woman to try again. Jean Shiley jumped first and made it. Babe also cleared the crossbar—this time without kicking it down next to herself in the pit.

The American teammates Jean and Babe were tied for the gold medal. Both expected the judges to lower the bar for another round of competition. Instead the judges huddled near the pit, talking about Babe's jumping form. Babe had been using the western roll, and they thought her head had gone over the bar before her feet. They said she had dived, which was not allowed. After a while they announced Babe was disqualified. The gold medal would be given to Jean Shiley, who later said she had wanted to complain about Babe's jumping style after every jump that day.

Babe protested her disqualification. She told the judges she had been jumping the same way all afternoon and asked them why she hadn't been disqualified before. Babe then stormed from the infield.

Sportswriters took Babe's side. From the pressbox her attempt looked legal to them. They argued in their newspapers that Babe had a right to continue jumping against Jean Shiley until one of them missed fair and square. But despite these protests, the judges stuck

to their decision. They awarded Babe "only" the silver medal for second place. Coast to coast, the newspaper headlines now praised her.

3 MEDALS FOR BABE
WORLD'S GREATEST WOMAN ATHLETE

Two golds and a silver. Babe flew back to Texas a hero. The city of Dallas gave her a parade big enough for the entire U.S. team. Twelve bands marched and played. Admiring people filled the car Babe rode in with roses and her hair with confetti. In her hometown of Beaumont, the high school band was called from its summer vacation to welcome her. Babe's parents sat beside her in the fire chief's car from the airport to their little house where Babe once won all the marbles. At last she had the fame she'd trained for all these years.

4

Living for Sports and Making a Living

Fame, yes. Fortune, no.

Babe had been competing for medals and trophies because only a professional athlete could take money prizes. Under the AAU rules, she was also not allowed to take gifts from fans. She could not take sports clothes or equipment or anything else for being in advertisements. If she broke a rule she ran a chance of being caught, and if that happened there would be a stiff penalty handed out to her from the Amateur Athletic Union.

Now—suddenly—Babe owned a car, a beautiful new red Dodge to drive around Dallas.

She was back at Employers Casualty in the fall of 1932. But on her salary alone she could not have afforded a car costing $835. The AAU asked her how she had paid for the Dodge. She explained that she was making car payments from her salary. They doubted her yet they left her alone until they discovered Babe's photograph in Dodge advertisements. Then the AAU dropped her from amateur competition. Babe reacted by claiming her name had been used without her permission. When she supplied letters from the Dodge dealer to support what she had said, the AAU reinstated her to full membership. That is, until Babe herself decided to "turn pro."

She frankly wanted to make more money than she could as a secretary. Her family needed constant help from her. Besides giving them a large part of her salary, Babe bought her mother and father expensive gifts. By becoming a professional, Babe would also be able to pay for the costly health care her parents were beginning to need.

Yes, Babe would willingly turn to a life in professional sports. But what sport?

There were no professional leagues for women who played basketball or baseball, Babe's team games. Track meets were for amateurs only. Babe played tennis and golf but not well enough to challenge nationally ranked players; and besides, there were few professional tournaments for women in either of these country-club sports.

Babe decided to go "on stage." She would become a performer of sports instead of a competitor. Over the next two years she put together an assortment of her athletic skills, added her brash tone of voice, shined up her harmonica, and toured America showing off.

At a theater in Chicago, Babe sang a popular song in a costume that included high heels, then slipped them off and sprinted as fast as she could on a treadmill to show her running form. She demonstrated her golf-driving form by hitting plastic balls into the audience. To end this goofy act, she played popular songs on her harmonica. She played songs again at an auto show in Detroit where she also signed autographs in the Dodge booth. (She may have taken their car as a gift, but this can't be known for sure.) Then in New York she starred in an exhibition basketball game. For a fee of $400 she helped beat a rough team named the Long Island Ducklings, whose players deliberately set out to foul the famous Babe Didrikson. They managed to rip her uniform.

"There's nobody who wants to win more than I do. But I've never played rough or dirty," Babe said about the game. She managed to be the high scorer even with Ducklings hanging all over her.

People bought tickets to her exhibitions because

they wanted to see a real live "folk hero." Newspapers had given Babe this tag after the Olympics, and she lived up to it. She entertained by shooting trick baskets and by speeding around the baseball field to slide headfirst home. Some reporters continued praising Babe as an athlete but others began to slip in words like "freakish" and "unfeminine" about her show business games.

Babe ignored her critics. She wanted to make money, even if it meant performing in sports that grown women were ridiculed for playing. Longer and longer trips took her to cities all over America.

She played exhibition basketball on a team made up of both men and women: Babe Didrikson's All-Americans. For $1,000 a month (a huge salary for a woman in those days) Babe traveled with her team from Iowa to Kansas to Nebraska, then north and east as far as Connecticut. She sent nearly all this money home. She went to Florida to be guest star in spring baseball camps. There she mingled with great players and pitched against real-live Red Sox, Dodgers, and Cardinals. She collected $200 for pitching only one inning per game. She sent most of this money home to her parents and to her savings account. After spring training she drove her own car from state to state to play for an all-male baseball team. She would pitch one or two innings, take a turn at bat, hop into her car, and drive to another small town in her 200-game schedule.

Babe loved to drive her car. Driving was another sport to her. She bought bigger and bigger cars, one after another, and traveled in comfort. Even so, she still saved most of her earnings.

Babe loved an audience, loved their attention. In front of any crowd she was at ease and pleasant. She joked and took a joke well, all the time realizing that many of her fans had paid to see Babe the clown and circus performer rather than Babe the athlete. She gave them their money's worth of both Babes.

Also, Babe loved meeting and talking to the famous male athletes who sometimes played against her or on the same teams. She became friends with Babe Ruth. She made it her habit to question professionals,

to pick up tips about the show business side of sports.

Yet most of all Babe loved competition. She missed the day-to-day excitement of matching her skills against the best players: really matching, not just showing off her form. The gifts from fans, the cheering, the travel, and lots of money were not enough to make Babe completely happy. For that she would need to test herself against the best. All she had to do now was decide on the right sport.

Babe chose golf.

Then in the next years she managed to make golf not just the right sport but the perfect competition for herself.

Already she could drive a golf ball 250 yards, an excellent distance for a slender (115 pounds) woman—an excellent distance even for a man, for that matter.

Babe had learned the basic golf shots from her Beaumont High School coach and had practiced them in Dallas every now and then. While in Los Angeles for the Olympics, Babe had been invited to play one day with four well-known reporters. They raved about the distance of her drives. In a newspaper column the next day Babe read that she "possessed the ability to be a great player."

Perhaps this comment inspired Babe to continue improving. Or perhaps she was attracted to golf as a way to spend her life outdoors, away from an office. Just exactly why Babe chose to make golf her main sport can only be guessed at. She was tired of team

life, certainly. She had never made lasting friends among her teammates. Probably, too, Babe believed that in the long run she could earn more money from golf (advertising golf clubs, starring in golf instruction films) than in her show business games. Also her reputation as an athlete was fading.

"My name had meant a lot right after the Olympic games but it had sort of been going down since then. I had to find some way to build my name again," she admitted.

Babe knew that golf skills would be difficult to master. Most golfers she would compete against had learned the basic movements when they were children. The swings for the many different clubs had to be flowing and natural. The rhythms of driving the

golf ball, chipping, and putting could rarely be added in later life to the basic athletic vocabulary of throwing, jumping, and running, not even with thousands of hours of practice.

Never mind what Babe knew about the physical barriers against reaching her goals. Her own body told her she could be the best with hard work—and Babe loved hard work.

She set about to practice more than she had on all her other sports combined. When she wasn't on the road playing exhibitions with her ball teams, she lived on her savings and hit golf balls. She sometimes arrived at a golf driving range at 5:00 A.M. to start hitting her 1,500 balls that day. She gripped her golf clubs the same way she held a baseball bat. This grip gave her swing a wonderful power but not the accuracy to win tournaments against women who had been playing golf most of their lives.

Fortunately Babe attracted teachers who took an interest in her game. "She was a warm and honest person. I liked her right away," one of her teachers said about Babe. "Her hands would blister up and bleed. She wore tape on them all the time," he added, to show how hard Babe practiced.

Babe learned to look at the ball during every move she made. She learned to keep her left arm firm and to stretch her fingers along the club instead of wrapping her hands into fists. These changes improved her swing.

To win golf tournaments, Babe had to drive her golf ball from the tees to a small hole under a flag that was 300, 400, 500 or more yards away from her. She had to putt her golf ball into those holes with as few swings (strokes) of her clubs as possible. The lower her score, the better the game she was playing.

In the fall of 1934 Babe decided to test her progress by playing in her first tournament. She chose the Fort Worth (Texas) Invitational, a small tournament close to where she was living in Dallas. She won the first round with a score of 77 for eighteen holes of golf. She was WONDERGIRL again in the newspapers.

BABE THE UNBEATABLE

But the very next day she lost, playing against a better golfer.

A Babe Didrikson loss! It did nothing to shake her determination. She would practice longer: sixteen hours a day. She'd practice indoors. She'd putt on a rug. She'd watch her swing over and over in a mirror preparing for the next tournament she had chosen to play, the Texas Women's Amateur Championship.

The sports world and Babe had almost forgotten she was no longer an amateur athlete.

5

At Home on the Golf Course

"The course was soggy. In spite of all the wetness I started off as if I was going to set the course on fire."

Babe wrote that about her first round of golf at the Texas Women's Amateur in April 1935. She continued her low scores round after round, to win handily.

"I was on top of the world. It had taken me longer than I originally figured to get going in golf, but I was rolling at last."

She had beaten a field of women who were almost her exact opposites. They were rich, older, long-time golfers from Texas country clubs. Many of them protested when Babe was allowed to enter "their " tournament; she just wasn't from the proper family background. They were grimfaced when they lost. Looking ahead to other tournaments, they saw Babe a winner for a long time to come. After all, she was only twenty-three years old. One of these women complained that because Babe was a professional in other sports she was also a professional golfer and should not be allowed to play in amateur tournaments.

The United States Golf Association agreed. It banned Babe from future amateur tournaments, saying they were doing it "for the best interest of the game."

Babe felt the bottom drop out of her life. All her practice! All her plans swept aside in what male golfers called "the dirtiest deal . . . in a long time" and "the biggest joke of the year." These men had their professional tournaments to play, but in those days there were almost no professional tournaments for women. Babe had lost her competition again.

No use griping about it, Babe convinced herself after weeks of trying to regain her amateur rating. She gave up writing letters to the golf association and began playing exhibition golf in foursomes with men, from whom she continued to learn. She brushed off the frequent rude comments from women members of country clubs where she played. No one ever heard Babe make a mean reply. Rather, she was sunny—and devilish—in front of crowds.

"You all come closer now. Today you're looking at the best," Babe would begin. She'd entertain with 300-yard drives. "Boy! Don't you men wish you could hit a ball like that?" she would ask. She would also hit trick shots. She could put her foot in front of the ball, hit the ball, and make it pop over her foot and into the cup. She'd hit left-handed. She'd startle on-lookers with her match trick: She secretly placed a kitchen match next to her teed-up ball. When she drove the ball from its tee, the match ignited, sounding like a cannon.

To blend in with her country club setting, Babe began wearing dresses. She curled her short hair. Eventually she let her hair grow longer. But she still refused to wear a girdle and stockings, not for anyone.

Babe saved her earnings, and when she had enough in the bank to make a move she took her father, mother, sister Lillie, and brother Arthur to Los Angeles. Babe liked California, with its happy memories of the Olympics. And her golf teacher lived there. She practiced her shots with him and gave exhibitions and occasionally entered tournaments that would let her play, including men's tournaments. At one of these, the Los Angeles Open ("open" to professionals along with amateurs) Babe played in a threesome that included the famous wrestler, George Zaharias.

It was practically love at first sight for both Babe and George. Soon Babe and George were going everywhere together—if their schedules allowed. George Zaharias wrestled professionally all over the United States. He was a large, handsome man who had grown up in a poor Greek-American family but who was now wealthy from investing his sports earnings. George and Babe were married in December 1938.

Babe Didrikson Zaharias. She spent her six-month honeymoon touring Australia with George. He continued to wrestle but also became manager of Babe's career. He arranged for her to give golf clinics and play exhibition rounds in Australia. She made fans of Australian newsmen by coming within two strokes of beating the Australian men's professional champion. That was juicy news.

A MAGNIFICENT SPECIMEN OF
ATHLETIC WOMANHOOD

is what one reporter called Babe in his column about her golf games.

Home in California, George encouraged his wife to try to get back her amateur standing as a golfer. George knew that Babe dreamed of playing tournament golf on the women's circuit. He offered his help toward Babe's dream.

She asked the United States Golf Association to

reinstate her as a member. They were willing to—if Babe would first go through a waiting period of three years. In that time, they told her, she must not take money for playing golf. She must not let advertisers use her name. These rules left Babe without an income. But, for a change, she had no worries. George supported her and also gave money to her family.

Babe's three years of waiting were joyous ones in the house George rented for them in Los Angeles. Babe had learned to cook and sew from her mother. Now she made George her Norwegian meatballs as well as his own favorite Greek dishes. She made shirts for George and curtains for their house on a sewing machine. She tended their flower garden, did the housework (without her scrub-brush skates!), and, of course, had time left over for her usual large share of sports. She took tennis lessons until she could beat her teacher. She took bowling lessons, achieving an average of 170 for a season in Los Angeles bowling leagues. To keep her eye sharp on the golf course, Babe played several times a week, often with Hollywood stars. George bowled and played golf with her. They were an outgoing couple who made friends almost everywhere they went.

The United States Golf Association returned Babe's amateur standing on January 21, 1943. "I don't think I've ever been happier in my life," she said. She was grateful to George. "He has done so much to boost my career along. I lean a lot on his advice. I listen to him about my golf playing, too."

Babe started winning tournaments as if she had been competing against the best women golfers all along. In 1945, after winning the Texas Women's Open and the women's Western Open (for the third time), she was voted the outstanding woman athlete of the year by Associated Press newsmen.

At the Western Open in June of that year, Babe persevered to the eighteenth hole of her final round despite the tragic phone calls she received before each round: Her mother was dying. Babe tried to leave Indiana for home, but airplanes and trains were filled with military passengers in wartime America. (World War II was in its last summer.) Babe walked around the golf course with tears in her eyes. Her mother wanted her to stay and play but she would rather have been at her mother's bedside. When she learned her mother had died, Babe found comfort in playing her harmonica for hours in her room. Next day she won the final match, for her momma.

Win after win after win after win after win—five tournaments in a row in the summer of 1946. Babe wanted to take a long layoff and stay home. But George looked ahead to history books. He had his own dream for Babe.

"Honey, you've got something going here. You want to build that win streak up into a record they'll never forget." George urged Babe to go to Florida for winter tournaments. She followed his advice, and after ten more wins without a defeat—fifteen wins in a row—George talked Babe into traveling all the way to Scotland to compete. If she won there she'd be the first American ever to win the British Women's Amateur.

Babe discovered herself the most popular golfer in Gullane, Scotland, from the moment she arrived. The Scots had been following her sports life in their newspapers. They knew all about the wonder girl. The hotel chef prepared Babe's favorite breakfast, including ham and bacon in a nation still suffering postwar shortages of meat. Strangers in the streets asked "Mrs. Zaharias" to tea. Townspeople delivered parcels of warm clothes to her hotel after she mentioned to newsmen she was cold in the damp weather.

Babe—the former tough kid from a poor family, the athletic "freak" in high school, the "muscle moll" to small minds critical of sportswomen—Babe was cherished in Scotland for her lifetime of striving to excel.

Her audience grew to thousands during her week at the British Amateur. People watched her from houses that lined the fairways. Babe posed for photos in kilts.

She sang a Scottish song and danced a highland fling. When she got far enough ahead of her opponents, Babe loosened up her fans with stunts, including her match trick that sounded like a cannon.

Several ladies complained about Babe's "show-off" behavior. A marshall on the course straightened them right out. "You are speaking of the finest woman golfer that has ever been here." To prove it, Babe won the tournament, the first American to do so.

It was win number sixteen in a streak of seventeen wins without a loss. No other golfer in the history of this sport—man or woman—has come near running up so long a streak.

Babe's final years of golf were fulfilling in ways other than simply winning tournaments. Her pride

and joy was the birth of the LPGA: the Ladies Professional Golf Association. With Babe's energy behind it, the LPGA soon had a well-organized golf tour with cash prizes for women who won. From then on, they wouldn't need to depend on their husbands or on others to support their "amateur" sports talent.

As a professional golfer, Babe became a millionaire. She liked that. She drove big fancy cars and ate steak. With her fame and her power over the LPGA she could call any country club home. She liked that. She liked and befriended many of her opponents on the tour. Many of them grew to like Babe in spite of—even because of—her high-spirited personality.

"Okay, Babe's here! Now who's gonna finish second?" she'd announce to begin a tournament.

Patty Berg, a fellow golfer, sometimes finished second, and once in a while finished ahead of Babe. She said about Babe, "She was the happiest girl you ever saw, like a kid. Our sport grew because of Babe, because she had so much flair and color. With Babe there was never a dull moment."

In 1954 Babe won five tournaments and was voted the Outstanding Athlete of the Year by the Associated Press for the *sixth* time in her life. Remarkable for any athlete at the "old" age of 43. But almost humanly impossible for Babe. She was dying of cancer. Typically she had ignored her early warnings, for athletes are used to playing when tired or when in pain. Thus her cancer spread beyond the control of doctors, one of whom warned that Babe would never play tournament golf again.

Three and a half months after surgery in 1953 Babe placed fifteenth in the All-American tournament. The following week she placed third in the World Golf championship. Babe missed many easy approach shots and short putts. She felt tired and shaky. George walked by her side with a seat for her to use during rests. Her golfer friend Betty Dodd traveled with Babe as her nurse, companion—and golf opponent.

In those last years Babe played in pain. She played to forget pain. She played confidently and well, adding to her growing reputation as the greatest athlete of the twentieth century.

Mildred "Babe" Didrikson Zaharias, 1911–1956.

ABOUT THIS BOOK

At the Babe Didrikson Memorial in Beaumont, Texas, you can see Babe's trophies and medals, her golf clubs and tennis racket, her high school yearbook and photographs from her scrapbooks.

If Texas is too far from your own sports turf, you can ride your bike to a library and bring Babe closer. Read the book she wrote about herself, *This Life I Led,* and read the wonderful biography *"Whatta-Gal": The Babe Didrikson Story.* It's fun to compare Babe's own boasts to the words of her family, her husband, friends, and competitors.

Test yourself against Babe's *measurable* abilities.

1. Warm up your throwing arm, and throw a baseball as far as you can. Measure your distance against Babe's throw of 272 feet 2 inches—almost the length of a football field.

2. Next, stand at the foul-shooting line on a basketball court. Take 65 foul shots in a row. Match your points to Babe's 57 out of 65.

3. At a golf-driving range, drive balls toward a sign marked 300 YARDS. Watch how close you come to Babe's drives, which were often as long as three end-to-end football fields.

I have taken these tests and others from Babe's record book during my own lifetime as an athlete. I've traveled to Beaumont to see Babe's Olympic medals and to run her streets. There I remembered myself as a young ballplayer, when girls with healthy batting averages were still called "freak." After years of roadblocks to being a professional athlete, I chose instead to write about them. Babe's genius was that *she played no matter what.*   R.R.K.